THE ADVENTURES OF
RUY DIVER

MIRIAM SALINAS

ILLUSTRATIONS BY: JOSHUA ALLEN

AuthorHouse™
1663 Liberty Drive
Bloomington, IN 47403
www.authorhouse.com
Phone: 1-800-839-8640

Published by AuthorHouse 5/29/2013

ISBN: 978-1-4817-5477-4 (sc)
ISBN: 978-1-4817-5478-1 (e)

Library of Congress Control Number: 2013909310

authorHOUSE®

For my beloved son, Ruy Benjamin,
And now for my dearest Ruy Matthew
And adorable Hugo Nicolas
And to Maribel Flores
for digging these wonderful
stories out of the drawer
and making this book happen…

RUY DIVER AND HIS FRIENDS

Once upon a time, there was a boy just like you. His name was Ruy. One day this little boy went to the beach. He knew nothing about the sea, but when he saw it, he shouted, "This is where I want to live forever and ever!"

Without thinking that he did not know how to swim, he jumped right into the middle of that big, blue water. He paddled his arms and kicked his feet, but he was sinking.

What was happening?

How terrifying!

Suddenly, it got dark all around him, as if someone had turned off the lights. He felt as though he was falling asleep. He thought he must have been asleep and that someone was gently rocking him in a huge hammock.

When he woke up, he was lying on soft, white sand, and the sun was drying the tiny water droplets on his body. He could not remember what had happened to him or why he was there. No one else was on the beach.

Suddenly, a lovely little voice asked, "How are you feeling?"

Ruy looked with amazement at a turtle. She wasn't big or small, but her eyes were beautiful—large and round, with long eyelashes—and she had a small, smiling mouth. Her face was framed by two long braids fastened at the tips with lacey strings of tiny seashells.

"How are you feeling?" she asked again.

The boy stared at her, doubting what he was hearing. A talking turtle? That happened only in storybooks.

"Would you like me to jump on your tummy again?" asked the turtle, concerned.

Ruy burst out laughing. How he laughed and laughed! When he caught his breath again, giggling, he asked, "Why do you want to jump on my tummy? Who are you? How is it that you can speak?"

The turtle understood that these were very reasonable questions and would answer them later. But now, it was more important to find out if the boy was really well. "Do you think you can walk to that palm tree?" she asked.

"Of course I can," answered the boy. And one step at a time they walked to the huge palm tree that had bunches of coconuts under the shady leaves.

"Who are you? How do you know how to speak?" asked Ruy again as he sat down, waiting for the turtle to arrive.

At last, she sat next to him. They looked out at the ocean, not far off.

"My name is Rosy. Rosy Turtle and yours?"

"My name is Ruy."

"Well, what a scare you gave us, Ruy. Fortunately my friends and I were playing in the shallows when you jumped in without a second thought."

"Believe me, Rosy Turtle, from now on and for the rest of my life, I will think twice before doing something so reckless."

Suddenly, something jumped out of the water, shouting, "How does he feel?" before diving back into the water.

Wide-eyed with surprise, Ruy asked Rosy, "Who was that?"

"That was Sally Snapper," she said.

Sally jumped into the air again. She was a darling fish, with long curls running down the length of her dorsal fin and lovely fluttering goo-goo eyes.

Ruy smiled and said, "Thank you, Sally."

"Sarah Sardine!" called out Rosy Turtle.

A silver arrow crossed the horizon. Sarah was swift and streamlined. Her small, lively eyes glimmered with fun. Just above her forehead, she wore a ribbon bow, embroidered with minute shells.

Ruy waved his hand and also thanked her. "Thank you, Sarah Sardine."

"Pete Pompano!" called Rosy again.

Pete tried to jump into the air as Sarah had done, but he only managed a huge flop and disappeared. Then he popped up his sleepy-eyed head and said, "Hi," in a very low and slow voice.

Ruy wanted to laugh, not **at** Pete, but **with** Pete, because he knew they would be friends forever. "Thank you, Pete Pompano," he said.

"Joey Fish!" Rosy Turtle continued calling.

Joey's head appeared, and Ruy saw his lovely beard, just a tuft under his mouth. "I can't jump out because I'm too fat. I love to eat," he said, embarrassed.

"Thank you, thank you, Joey Fish, and don't feel embarrassed with me. I love you just as you are," Ruy said tenderly.

"Octi Octopus!" cried Rosy.

The water started churning and foaming. Among the large and small bubbles, a long arm came out, then another, and another, until finally Octi's shiny head surfaced. He seemed to be very angry, and this unsettled Ruy.

Rosy Turtle said, "He looks angry, but he isn't. As a matter of fact, he was the one that held you in his arms so you wouldn't keep on sinking."

Ruy felt a knot in his throat as he thought about how this ugly fellow with such an angry expression, had saved his life. With tears in his voice, he said, "Thank you forever, dear friend."

Funny things happen in the ocean. Octi Octopus blushed like a tomato. He didn't need any thanking for what all octopuses do: hold on to anything falling.

"We all pulled you out," said Rosy Turtle, "but being the biggest of them all and because I can live out of the water, it was I who dragged you up to the beach."

Ruy took Rosy's hands in his, squeezing them tenderly. "Thank you, my dearest friend," he said, and he hugged her. Both let a few tears of joy drop in the sand because they already knew they would be friends forever and ever.

The entire group shouted with joy and began to sing a song:

Now we have a friend, a real friend.

This darling boy will always be a friend,

A real friend.

They kept on singing and shouting until Sarah Sardine, wanting more excitement, called out, "Let's teach him how to swim! We are all great swimmers. We can be the best teachers!"

"Yes! Yes! Yes!" they all shouted.

Uh-oh, Ruy felt a little scared. After what had happened to him, he wasn't very excited about getting in the water again.

Rosy Turtle took his hand, saying, "Don't be afraid. Sit right here in the shallow water and let the Ocean get to know you."

The little laps of water moved him back and forth, from side to side. Some of them, playfully, tried to pull him into deeper water, but they were only joking.

As Ruy and Rosy sat there, she explained this to him: "The Ocean is our mother and father because all life began in its waters. It is the Ocean that has given you the gift of speaking with us. This gift is very rarely given, only to those whose heart has been seen by the Ocean, to those who are good and brave."

Ruy was joyful and said, "Thank you, Ocean, for being so kind to me."

From far, far away, a deep, noble voice was heard. It was Ocean's voice that said, "Welcome home, Ruy Diver."

"A DIVER, He will be a diver!" shouted the group.

With his slow, deep, gruff voice, Pete Pompano said, "What joy, what happiness."

Joey Fish popped up, saying, "Come on, Ruy Diver. Let's go eat. I'm hungry."

Flirty Sally Snapper made goo-goo eyes at him, saying, "What are you waiting for? Start swimming!"

The boy let go of Rosy's hand, turning over on his tummy and paddling his legs.

Octi Octopus interrupted, "Your arms, Use your arms!",

"Look how I use them!" Octi spun his eight arms like a cartwheel.

Ruy tried to copy him but didn't manage to hold himself afloat.

"You will never learn to swim. You don't have enough arms," Octi said sadly.

Oh! Octi should never have said that. Ruy Diver felt his pride pinched. He waved his arms and plunged in the water, kicking up more water and bubbles than a fire hose, but he was floating!

In his slow, gruff voice, Pete Pompano contributed to the swimming class. "Kick your legs faster."

"If that fatso Joey Fish can swim, anybody can swim!" added another teacher.

"Go! Go! Go!" they encouraged him.

"Let the air out slowly when your head is in the water," they advised.

Suddenly, Ruy Diver was swimming like a champ. He dove down, came up for air, dove down again, and was soon doing all sorts of tricks underwater.

"Oh my, what great teachers we are!" they congratulated each other.

While all this was going on, Rosy Turtle watched Ruy's progress. When she saw that he could swim perfectly, she said, "You are now ready for the equipment."

"What equipment?" they all asked, surprised.

"The diver's equipment!" Air tanks, goggles, fins—how else is he going to see the submarine world?" she answered.

"Oh, I guess she's right," someone muttered.

"Where will we get that kind of equipment?" asked Sally Snapper.

Rosy Turtle felt so proud of herself when she said, "I know where to find some, left by the pearl fishermen. Let's go!"

And off they went.

In three shakes of a nanny goat's tail, they were back with the air tanks, fins and everything else that Ruy Diver would need.

The boy followed Rosy Turtle's instructions carefully. Although she was usually quite forgetful, this time Rosy remembered step-by-step what she had seen the pearl divers do.

Practice makes perfect, they say, and soon enough Ruy Diver was another fish in the mighty ocean. His friends pointed out for him which marine life was harmless and which could be dangerous. "Never touch a sea urchin. They are always in a bad mood," and "Jellyfish, the beauties of the sea! Never touch them! Their beautiful hair can hurt you badly," they told him.

They swam to Seashell Field, where everyone lived. Mr. and Mrs. Snapper kissed Rudy Diver's forehead warmly, saying, "Welcome home, sweetheart."

Mr. and Mrs. Octopus got tied up in their sixteen arms when they hugged him.

Mr. Fish and his wife brought all their family: uncles, cousins, sisters-in-law, sons, daughters-in-law, aunts, and godparents. They were all very fat and, like Joey, had little tufts of beards. They all chattered at the same time, complaining that Joey was too thin and asking if Ruy Diver could help him gain some weight.

Mr. Sardine, Sarah's dad, who was just as slim and streamlined as his daughter, whispered to Mrs. Sardine: "Joey is too fat already!" but dropped the subject and also kissed Ruy Diver on his cheeks.

The Pompano family stared at Ruy Diver with their huge, wide eyes, making him uncomfortable. He wondered if they saw something he could not see. Maybe he was growing a fish tail? Nope, nothing of the sort… Then the boy realized that this is the way Pompanos are, they stare. Mr. Pompano asked, "Do you like our world?"

Joyfully, Ruy hugged the family, at the same time crying out, "I am the happiest I've ever been!"

Then Rosy Turtle took Ruy Diver's hand and led him to her home, which was not far away.

He was right about that, because out of the sand wriggled a crooked, flattened, horribly squashed being. Ruy took the fish in his hands ever so carefully and, almost crying, said, "Look what I've done! Let's take him to the hospital!"

The fish coughed and coughed, spitting sand from his crooked mouth. Mr. Turtle saw that the fish was fine and burst out laughing. Even Rosy laughed.

"It's Eddie Sole! Don't worry, he's like that. He's crooked," she said.

Annoyed, Eddie Sole said, "That's what I get for disappearing in the sand," and coughed again.

Ruy set him down on the sea floor, saying, "I'm so sorry, Eddie Sole, for having stepped on you. Could we still be friends?"

"Of course!" said the fish emphatically. "Any friend of Rosy is my friend." And he dug himself into the sand again.

It was getting dark. They had been so happy that they hadn't realized that evening was just minutes away.

They all swam up to the beach. The boy had had a very full day and needed to sleep, in order to be bright-eyed and bushy-tailed the next day.

Lying on the sand, Ruy and Rosy watched the beautiful sunset.

"This is where I want to live forever," said Ruy Diver. "Tomorrow I will build a little house, right here on the beach, so I can be near all of you."

"I think that is a wonderful idea," said Rosy. "We will all help you make a lovely home. We will bring lovely seashells to hang on the walls. We will build a bench with wood from the sunken ship—" Rosy realized she was speaking to a deeply asleep boy. She covered him with warm sand and said, "Goodnight, Ruy Diver. See you tomorrow morning."

He heard her and, yawning, answered, "Goodnight, Rosy. See you tomorrow … and thank you again … good night, Ocean."

Rosy Turtle went back to her friends in the water, and they all watched how this wonderful boy slept.

Little by little, they all went home singing a soft lullaby:

Sleep tight
All night
We just might
Find we like
You more
Tomorrow night.

RUY DIVER AND HiS
FRiENDS BUiLD A HOUSE

The following morning, the sky shone before Mr. Sun showed up. The pinky rays tickled Ruy Diver's toes and eyelids until he opened his eyes.

How wonderful the ocean looked. It seemed like a thousand colored feathers were swimming on its surface. The tiny ripples of water by the edge raced up to Ruy's big toe and tickled it. Giggling, they raced back to their place, very proud of the joke they had played.

Ruy smiled and stood up. He yawned and said, "Good morning, Ocean."

"I'm hungry," he added.

Just then, his friends started jumping up from the water. "Good morning, good morning. We have brought your breakfast!" they cheered.

Belly flop after belly flop, Joey Fish insisted on showing his friend a bagful of oysters he brought.

Pete Pompano said, "I've brought you some clams."

Sarah Sardine kept jumping in the air, shouting, "Hurry, hurry, eat your breakfast. It's time to play!"

Soon enough, Rosy Turtle showed up dragging a big bunch of seaweed. "I chose the tenderest leaves for you," she said. "It's my favorite breakfast."

Ruy sat next to Rosy and stared at the seaweed. Rosy guessed he didn't like the idea of eating it.

"Have you ever tried it?" she asked.

"No," answered the boy.

"Then you don't even know what it tastes like. Just try it. If you absolutely don't like it, I will eat it," she said happily, thinking how lucky she would be to get a double ration, the one she had eaten earlier and this one. She smelled the seaweed with her tiny nose, and her mouth watered.

"That's like eating grass!" said Sarah Sardine. "Here! This is real food," she added, placing a net bag of plankton near Ruy's feet. "Hurry, eat it up, and let's go play!" she cried, and off she went.

Two crabs walked up on the beach dragging bags of oysters and clams. They said, "Good morning," and proceeded to open the shells.

Not so far away, Octi Octopus held a stone in one of his arms and started swinging it with all his strength, aiming at the palm trees. He let go of the stone, and it was a bull's eye shot. It hit the coconut, and down it came. The coconut rolled right up to one of the crabs, who quickly grabbed it in his claws and cracked it open.

Ruy Diver was about to take a sip of coconut water when Sarah Sardine stopped him. "Tssst, tssst, first drink your plankton!" she said firmly.

He wasn't going to get out of it, so he pinched his nose and drank up.

He didn't like it at all, and made faces. Sarah's feelings were hurt, but she mumbled, "You just wait and see how strong you'll feel."

And, oh, surprise! Immediately, he felt how a burst of strength started running up his muscles. He decided it was a matter of getting used to anything new.

While he was eating his oysters and clams, Rosy handed him some seaweed. "Go on, just try it," she said, smiling. Ruy was not going to hurt her feelings, so he tasted it. It wasn't that bad, but not delicious, so he didn't accept the second bunch she offered him.

"If you had to build a house, how would you build it?" the boy asked Rosy as they ate.

"Oh, what a wonderful question," she said. "Well, I would—" but she stopped in mid-sentence. All the importance she had felt a moment ago simply slipped away.

"I don't know, Ruy," she said unhappily.

"I need a home, Rosy. When the rains and storms come, how will I shelter myself? And I'll need a roof over my head in winter."

They walked along the beach in deep thought.

Sarah Sardine jumped up. "What's wrong? When are we going to play?"

"You only think about playing. Can't you see we are thinking?" said Rosy, a little bothered.

"What are you thinking about?" asked Sarah, unaware that Rosy was annoyed.

"We are thinking that Ruy Diver needs a house."

"Okay. He can come and live with me. Now, let's go play!" said Sarah.

"Oh, Sarah!" Rosy said. "Ruy can't live underwater all the time. Besides, your place is too small."

"You are absolutely right! Let's build him a house," said Sarah, ready to tackle the problem.

"Fine, but how?" asked Rosy Turtle.

"Well, let me think about that," said Sarah, who stopped jittering around while she thought.

Pete Pompano came by and asked, "What's up, Sarah?" in his deep, gruff voice.

"Ruy Diver needs a home," said Sarah.

"Oh, I see," said Pete, and he stayed next to Sarah, thoughtful.

Just then, Sally Snapper came up and asked, "What's wrong?" She was obviously concerned, seeing them all so quiet.

"Nothing is wrong. We are just thinking," they answered in unison.

"Thinking what?" Sally asked.

"That Ruy Diver needs a home," they answered.

"Oh, I see," said Sally, blinking her goo-goo eyes. And she also set herself to thinking.

Joey Fish came by (swimming with difficulty) and asked, "What are you all thinking?"

"We are thinking that Ruy Diver needs a home!" they shouted together. So Joey waddled next to them and also started thinking.

All at once, they turned their heads to see Octi Octopus, who was dragging and pulling something unbelievably heavy. He was sweating like an open hose.

"What on earth are you doing?" they asked, amazed at this strength.

"Can't you see? This is going to be Ruy Diver's home," he said, quite exhausted.

"A whale's skeleton?" They inquired in absolute amazement.

"You'll see. Give me a hand, you lazy bones," he ordered.

They all promptly obeyed and pushed and pulled and dragged, and pushed and pulled and dragged again.

When Ruy Diver saw the huge whale skeleton appear on the beach, he gave a somersault of sheer joy.

"Rosy, my home! My home!" he shouted.

"It's a monster! Oh me, oh my, it's a monster! Hurry, we must hide!" Rosy whimpered in terror and dug herself into the sand.

Ruy Diver ran toward the skeleton and pulled with all his strength until it rested on the beach.

Rosy Turtle peeked out from under the sand and was almost in tears. "My poor friend!" she said. "Oh, my poor friend, with that breakfast we gave him, he's lost his marbles. That monster is going to catch him!" Rosy was truly in despair.

However, seeing that the monster moved only when Ruy pulled it, she poked her head out and then, little by little, crawled out of her hideout. A moment later, she was pushing the whale's rib cage until it sat right under the palm tree.

The group of friends cheered from the water while Ruy Diver looked at his future home with his arms akimbo, imagining it ready for his first night in his very own place.

No one lost time. They all rushed out and returned with what they thought was lovely. There was an uncomfortable moment when they started arguing about how to decorate the place. But Octi settled the issue by telling them that, as the great-great grandson of the most admired architect Tobias Octopus, it was his right to direct the building and decoration. No one opposed this decision. He was right, as usual.

The house was finished at about noon. How beautiful it looked! Ruy Diver had placed fallen palm leaves over the whale's backbone, shading and protecting the interior. The crabs cut off banana leaves and placed them on the floor like carpets. Strings of shells made music with the breeze. A giant clamshell had been placed in the corner, to be used as a bathtub. On top of the whale's back they placed another giant clamshell to collect the evening dew and rainwater, which would be nicely warmed by the sunshine whenever Ruy wanted to take his daily bath.

Ruy came out on the porch wearing his scuba equipment and jumped into the sea. They all greeted him with cheers.

Pete Pompano said in his deep, gruff voice, "I want to live with you, Ruy Diver."

"No! No! No!" said Joey Fish. "*I* want to live with you!"

"And just how do you think you're going to do that?" asked Sarah Sardine, who was smarter than she looked. "You and you," she said, pointing at Pete and Joey, "are fish! And fish can't live out of the water," she concluded, feeling very wise.

A very proud and satisfied Octi Octopus said, "The house isn't finished yet. It needs a bed." They all looked at each other and agreed.

"There are several beds in the sunken ship. If you give us a hand, Ruy, we can take one out."

So, off they went to the sunken ship. Soon enough, they reached the huge, dark shadow of what had been the Black Pirate's ship, resting at the bottom of the ocean. They went in through a window. It was deadly quiet. When the fish talked, a deep echo carried their voices on and on. The deeper they went into the bowels of the ship, the darker it became. Suddenly, they were apart, and Ruy Diver found himself all alone. He wasn't scared. He had always been brave and fearless, and he felt very excited to be walking through the same places that many pirates had walked before.

He entered a spacious room where thousands of colorful sea anemones swayed with the current. There was a large trunk in a corner. What could be in it? He opened it, with creaks and groans. By Neptune's beard! What was he seeing?

A million flashes of unbelievable rainbow colors made him close his eyes for a second. Then, he saw the jewels: crowns and rings, necklaces and bracelets, gold coins. Everything sparkled: gold and silver set with precious stones, rubies and emeralds, diamonds and sapphires. It was an incredible treasure.

Suddenly, Ruy felt he was not alone. Someone else was there, watching him. He felt the presence come closer, and when he bolted to see who or what it was, a blackish shadow fell upon him. He was being shoved into a sack and carried away.

He wanted to feel scared, but he did not think that would help. He had to think how to get out of there.

Moving around inside the sack, he examined it part by part and soon found a little hole. Quickly he pulled and stretched it, making it bigger.

In the meantime, in another part of the sunken galleon, his friends were looking for him.

"We found it! We found your bed!" they called and called. "Ruy Diver, where are you?"

Little did they know what had happened to him. They continued looking everywhere, up and down, from side to side, until they came upon a very upset and angry Eddie Sole. He was desperately trying to say something but could only flip up and down in his panic.

"What is it? Speak up!" shouted Sally Snapper.

In his alarmed, gruff voice, Pete Pompano demanded, "You saw something. Speak up!"

"Silly, silly Eddie Sole, please say something," pleaded the nervous Sarah Sardine.

As usual, it took level-headed Octi Octopus to calm everyone down while Rosy Turtle soothed Eddie.

"There, there, darling," she coaxed Eddie Sole. "We are here to help. Did you see something frightening? Is Ruy Diver in danger?"

Eddie was so angry he only blurted out, "Filbert Shark!" and pointed the way he had seen Filbert swim with the sack on his back. They all headed in that direction as fast as they could.

Meanwhile, Ruy Diver had made a hole large enough to crawl out of the sack.

What would you have done if you saw a shark with an empty sack on his back?

Well, Ruy Diver did not run away. Instead, he shouted, "Coward! Come and get me if you can!"

The shark stopped swimming. He looked at his sack and then at Ruy, who stood his ground with clenched fists pointed at the shark.

Filbert Shark dropped the sack and came closer, squinting his eyes. He could not understand what had happened. When he was closely looking through his squinting eyes at Ruy Diver, the boy let go of a fist, smacking the shark on the tip of his nose.

"Oh, oh, oh, oh, you hit me! I'm going to tattle on you!" whimpered the shark as he sat rubbing his nose, while tiny tears trickled from his nearly blind eyes.

Ruy was taken aback. He was ready for a good fight. Just then, Octi Octopus grabbed him protectively with his eight arms. Sally Snapper, Sarah Sardine, and Rosy Turtle placed themselves between the boy and the weeping shark, while Joey Fish, Pete Pompano, and Eddie Sole formed a barrier, facing Filbert.

"What were you up to, Filbert Shark?" they demanded.

Filbert stopped sobbing and whimpered, "I was only playing a joke on him. I wasn't going to hurt him."

Octi Octopus let go of Ruy Diver, who assured him he was fine and not to worry. He approached Filbert in a calm but serious way. "Is that what you consider a joke? To come up behind my back and shove me into a sack, without an explanation of what you're going to do? Well, your idea of a joke is NOT a joke!" he said.

Filbert Shark hung his head and tearfully explained himself: "I only wanted to meet you. Yesterday, when everybody was introduced to you, nobody cared about me, and I, too, am a creature of the sea." This time, huge tears were dripping from his eyes into the water.

"Crybaby," said Pete Pompano in his deep, slow voice.

"And a trickster!" accused Sarah Sardine.

"And you play very bad jokes!" added Sally Snapper.

"That's why we don't want you as a friend!" topped off Joey Fish.

But Ruy Diver approached Filbert Shark with an open hand. "If you promise not to play bad jokes from now on, I will be your friend," he offered.

"No! No! No! No!" they all shouted.

"I'm sorry," said Ruy Diver very decidedly, "but if you all are my friends, Filbert is also my friend." He shook hand and fin with the smiling, happy shark.

Sharks look funny when they smile, sort of lamb-like. That's how Filbert Shark looked when he said, "Thank you, Ruy Diver. My friend!" implying that the boy was friends with only him—and with no one else.

Then, everybody shook fins with Filbert Shark. When they all saw each other's angry faces, they burst out laughing.

Now, a more pressing problem was at hand: getting Ruy Diver's bed into his home. They all swam back to the sunken ship, and with the help of Filbert Shark's size and strength, they dragged the bed out and carried it to the beach.

Once the bed was inside the whale's skeleton, Rosy Turtle and Ruy gathered the bird feathers that were lying around and made a very comfy mattress.

Again, it was time for the sun to set. It would soon be bedtime. Ruy walked Rosy to the edge of the water, where they said goodnight. Ruy raised his hand and waved at all the fish, saying, "Tomorrow we will play all day long!"

He watched as the stars began to twinkle, and he yawned. He was very tired. "Good night, Ocean," he said and entered his home.

He sank into the feathers and closed his eyes, thinking about his friends. The soft sea breeze swung the shells making music while Ruy fell asleep.

SOMEONE ELSE LIVES IN RUY DIVER'S HOME

Well, Ruy Diver's first night in his whale-skeleton home was not that peaceful.

He was so tired from all the fuss caused by Filbert Shark that he could not fully wake up to figure out what was not letting him fall asleep.

However, the next morning all he could remember was the sound of sad crying, as if a child were weeping at the bottom of a well.

That's silly, thought Ruy. *No one else is here except me.* Yet, he couldn't dismiss from his mind what sounded like the sad whimpering of a young boy.

He went out on his porch and absently said, "Good morning, Ocean."

The little waves answered, "Good morning," and were surprised to see Ruy put his diver's suit on without eating breakfast. Last evening's events made him lose his appetite.

"Morning!," said Sarah Sardine. "Here's your plankton. Hurry up and let's go play."

"Hello, hello," said Rosy Turtle. "My aunt Cookie sent you two turtle eggs. Here they are."

"I'm not really hungry," Ruy said distractedly.

The crabs dragged up their bags of oysters and clams and immediately started opening them.

"What's wrong?" asked Rosy.

"You won't believe this," answered Ruy.

"What?"

"Well, I think that someone else is living in my home."

"What!" exclaimed Rosy, wide-eyed. "I was the last one to leave last night, and there was no one else."

Sarah Sardine, Pete Pompano, and Joey Fish came up closer to listen to the conversation. Seeing he had company, Ruy decided to have his breakfast and tell them about the previous evening.

"I was so tired I fell like a log on the feathers of my bed," he said.

"Me, too," interrupted Pete.

Along came Octi Octopus, saying, "Hi, Ruy."

"Maybe you can help me figure out what's happening in my home," said Ruy. "I was so tired, I just fell asleep."

"Me, too," Pete interrupted again.

The group gave Pete Pompano dirty looks, meaning, "You shut up or beat it!" and then looked at Ruy expectantly.

"Well, I know I was asleep … but I kept hearing someone, a kid, crying and sobbing," he told them.

"Oh, how spooky!" said Pete Pompano, wide-eyed.

Sarah Sardine swam up to Sally Snapper, who was just arriving, and, very scared, whispered in her ear: "A little boy cries in Ruy Diver's home."

"What did you have for breakfast, Sarah? That's nonsense, absolute nonsense," Sally said.

"Quiet, please. Let Ruy Diver tell us what happened," said the ever-thoughtful Octi Octopus.

They all kept still, looking at Ruy in expectation.

"That's all," he said, calmly.

"What do you mean, 'That's all'? It's horrible!" said Sarah, very frightened.

"Yes, that's all," repeated Ruy.

"Nightmares, maybe?" asked Octi, who always wanted everything clearly spelled out.

"No. I asked myself the same while fast asleep. Actually, I dreamed of wonderful things. I dreamed we were playing baseball."

"Oh, what fun!" shouted Sally Snapper.

"Yes, yes, let's play baseball!" said Pete.

"I want to be first!" said Octi Octopus, already forgetting what they had been talking about.

"Excuse me, but what is baseball?" said a curious Rosy Turtle.

"Do you know what baseball is?" Sally Snapper asked Joey Fish.

"I don't. Do you?" answered Joey, very matter-of-fact.

Then, they all looked at Ruy Diver for an explanation.

"I'll show you right now!" said Ruy, and he went to his home. He came back with a bat and a ball.

They knew about balls, but what was that wooden stick for?

"We have to make up two teams," Ruy explained.

"Me first! Me first!" insisted Octi Octopus.

"Wait. First we must have a toss," said Ruy.

"A toss?" asked Pete.

"You are sooo dumb, Pete Pompano!" exclaimed Sarah Sardine impatiently. "Yes, a toss," she added.

Sally gave her a suspicious look with her goo-goo eyes. "What is a toss?" she asked, innocently.

"Well, a toss … a toss is …" Sarah thought and thought and came up with the only thing she really knew something about. "A toss is a speed race. The one that gets there first, wins!" she finished.

"Oh!" said Sally Snapper, quite convinced.

"No, not at all," said Ruy, taking a coin out of his pocket. "This is a toss," and he flipped the coin and showed them what was "heads" or "tails."

Everything about the crying, whimpering voice of a boy at Ruy Diver's house was forgotten, and off they went to the Pearly Fields.

Once there, they made up the two teams, not without arguing about Octi having eight arms and whether that had to be taken into account.

Rosy was on first base. "Lightning" Sarah Sardine was fielder, and Joey Fish was the catcher. It was Octi Octopus's turn at the bat. Sally threw a perfect pitch, and Octi swung with all his arms. The ball flew, flew, flew, and was gone.

Rosy made her first homerun, followed by a very fast Octi. Two homeruns!

Joey Fish threw his mitt down, saying he wasn't playing anymore. Ruy Diver called out, "Where's the ball? We've only had two strikes."

Sarah Sardine was zipping back and forth, around and around, looking for the ball. It was nowhere to be seen. They all went to help find it. They overturned stones and seashells and removed seaweed. Nothing... No sign of the ball. It was as if a shark had swallowed it.

They were digging in the sand when Eddie Sole popped up.

"Can't a fellow have a peaceful rest without someone coming along and upsetting his home?" he shouted. "I pick the loneliest place on the sea floor to make my home, and you all come and make a mess of it." Would you like *me* to mess up your homes, your beds and your kitchens?" he continued, really angry.

"Sorry," said the group, with downfallen heads.

"Why do you do it to *me?*" Eddie demanded, almost in tears.

"Eddie, you keep changing addresses, and you don't even let us know where you'll be next," Sally said.

"What should I do about that?" he said, getting angrier. "Maybe hang a poster saying, 'Eddie doesn't live here anymore. He's over there, and tomorrow he'll be over there'?"

It was time for Ruy Diver to intervene. "Sorry Eddie, We are really sorry, but Octi hit a terrific homerun, and the ball ended up somewhere around here. We were only looking for the ball."

"Oh, I guess we should have started there," said Eddie, as if nothing had happened. "I saw Filbert Shark hiding behind those rocks over there," he said and pointed to a mound.

"That's all we needed!" they sighed. "Just when we are winning, he pulls one of his pranks," said a very annoyed Octi Octopus.

Pete Pompano was so angry he blew himself up like a balloon, and he wasn't even a puffer fish. "If I find him, I'm going to sock it to him!" he blurted. The whole group stared at Pete, because he was the most laid-back fish in the ocean.

"But he's our friend," said an incredulous Ruy. "Why would he do something like this?"

"Oh, you don't know him. He's famous for his horrible pranks, and this is a Filbert Shark prank," said Rosy.

Joey Fish added, "Let's go find him. Maybe he didn't take the ball. Let's give him a chance."

Off they went to Filbert's house. They reached the dark cave; it did not look inviting. Who would be the brave one to knock at the door? They looked at each other.

"Go on, Pete. You knock and when he opens the door, you sock it to him," said Sally, with scared goo-goo eyes.

Pete Pompano looked at them all with his big, round eyes, hoping someone would hold him back, and went to nestle himself in Ruy Diver's arms. "Hold me back, Ruy, hold me back, 'cause I could hurt Filbert!" he said.

"Well, I'm not scared of him," said Rosy Turtle. "Not of him or his mom or dad," and she went up to knock at the door.

Mrs. Shark opened the door. When Pete saw Filbert's mom, he jumped out of Ruy's arms and quickly hid behind the boy's air tanks.

"Good morning, kids. Can I help you?" she asked very kindly.

Octi Octopus was taken aback by her kind tone, but he felt he should be the spokesperson to address the problem. "Well, Mrs. Shark, you see … well, we're looking for Filbert," he finally blurted.

"I'm so sorry, kids, but he just went out to play with the ball you so kindly gave him. Thank you all for being so nice to him," she said, looking at each and every one of them through her tiny, almost blind eyes. "Who is Ruy Diver?" she asked.

"I am," said the boy, advancing toward her.

"I'm so pleased to meet you. Filbert told me you are his friend."

"Yes, ma'am, we are friends."

"Tell her about the ball," whispered all the fish behind him.

Ruy whispered back under his breath, "We aren't tattletales. This is between Filbert and us."

"It's been a pleasure to meet you all, and you are welcome to our home. Come again and play with our precious Filbert. Now, I must go back to my chores. Bye-bye, kids," she said and closed the door.

"Sooo, we *gave* him the ball!" said Octi Octopus.

"What a liar!" said Sarah Sardine, quite disgusted.

"Not only a liar, but a thief as well," concluded Sally Snapper, shaking her curls.

"Let's go look for him and teach him a lesson," suggested Joey Fish.

This time, they headed to the Lagoon Fields and found Filbert Shark playing with the ball and talking to himself: "Losers weepers, finders keepers, now I have the ball!"

"That ball belongs to us!" they shouted, giving him a good scare.

He hadn't seen them coming, so it scared the willies out of him—so much so that he fell on his back, all the while clasping the ball to his chest.

"It's mine! I found it!" he screamed.

Ruy Diver knew they would quarrel and quickly said, "Just a minute, Filbert. Who gave you that ball?"

Filbert Shark peered at Ruy through his tiny nearly blind eyes and said, "A friend gave it to me."

"Why did you say you found it? We all heard you say that," argued Ruy Diver.

"I did find it! Well, no … a friend gave it to me," answered Filbert.

"Your mom just told us that you said we had given it to you. Is this the truth?" asked Ruy.

Filbert lowered his head and began to cry.

"Nobody loves me!" he whimpered. "No one wants to play with me."

They all felt bad seeing those big tears rolling down Filbert's tiny eyes.

"Filbert," said Ruy, swimming right up to him, "all we want to know is why you took the ball."

"You don't like me. No one invited me to play with you. If I can't play, no one's going to play!" finished the shark.

Octi Octopus felt like squeezing him with his eight arms, he was so angry. All the rest squinted their eyes at him, as if to say, "Oh, you nasty shark!"

However, Ruy Diver said calmly, "We didn't include you, Filbert, 'cause you weren't around when the teams were organized. If you saw us, why didn't you join us? We would have gladly included you."

Filbert brushed his tears away with his fins and then smiled that sheepish smile of his and said, "I thought taking the ball would be a fun prank."

"A prank!" exclaimed Sally Snapper indignantly. "Of course, you and your pranks!"

Sarah Sardine, who was the angriest of them all because she hadn't had a chance to hit the ball, said, "It's your fault that we couldn't finish the game! It's getting dark now, and we've all got to go home."

"Oh, no!" said Rosy Turtle. "Just when it was our turn at the plate."

"Can I play with you all tomorrow?" asked an anxious Filbert Shark.

"Not a bad idea," said Pete Pompano. "That would even out the teams, four and four."

Filbert was so happy he jumped up twice and did a somersault.

They all went back to the beach, where Ruy Diver said goodnight.

The water in his clamshell tub was nice and warm. After the bath, Ruy put on his pajamas and dived into his feather bed, thinking about the next day's fun.

He was just about to fall asleep when he heard a sad, deep whimpering.

"Boooooo hooooo, boooooo hooooo."

He wasn't dreaming that much he knew. Or maybe he was! He opened his eyes wide and rolled them from side to side without moving his head.

Again, the voice whimpered a little louder: "Boooooo hooooo, booooo hooooo." It seemed to come from right under him. Slowly, he turned his head toward the feathers and tried to see what was there out of the corners of his eyes. But it was just as dark as night.

"Booooo hooooo. Oh, oh, oh, oh," said the voice.

Ruy jumped out of bed faster than a lightning bolt.

What would you have done if you had heard a low, deep whimpering from under your bed?

Well, Ruy Diver was a very brave boy and started digging into the feathers, throwing them up in the air, so that pretty soon it looked like a snowstorm. And what do you think he found?

A little ghost lying down!

He was the cutest little ghost anyone had ever seen, even if big tears were rolling from his eyes.

"Why are you crying?" asked Ruy.

"I can't get out of here," answered the little ghost.

"Why are you there?" asked the boy.

"Well … this is my bed!" said the ghost.

"What do you mean, this is your bed? We took it out from the sunken ship yesterday, and no one lives there."

"I live in that ship, and this is my bed!" the little fellow insisted. "I am the son of the Black Pirate, in case you didn't know."

"Sorry. I didn't know. Where's your dad?" asked Ruy.

"He and the other pirates swam away when the ship started sinking, and as I was sound asleep in this bed, I just stayed," explained the ghost.

"Should I believe you?" asked Ruy Diver, a bit suspicious about this wild story.

"Oh, it's true! I promise it's true. And I am really happy you took my bed out from the sunken ship. I was getting really bored playing in the same place for three hundred years. It stops being fun, you know? Now I can play here, if you let me," he added with his sweetest, nicest smile.

"Be my guest!" said Ruy. "But tell me, why were you whimpering last night and tonight, just when I lay down?"

"Do you think you're weightless? You would also cry if someone squashed you with a huge stone!"

Ruy Diver laughed. "Why didn't you speak up?"

"I didn't know it was you. There were so many feathers piled up on me. What's your name?" asked the little ghost.

"My name is Ruy Diver. And yours?" said Ruy.

"My name is Plutarch Ignatius Francis Anthony Sebastian," answered the ghost.

"Oh, boy! What a fancy name!" Ruy said with eyes wide.

"That's exactly what I told my dad, the Black Pirate. But he said that was my name, so that's it," said the ghost, a bit unhappy.

"It's a bit too long to say every time I have to introduce you to my friends. Imagine me saying, 'Rosy Turtle, this is Plutarch Ignatius Francis Anthony Sebastian.' That will take me five minutes to say," complained Ruy.

"You are so right. Why don't you give me a new name?" asked the ghost.

Ruy Diver thought it over a moment and then said, "How about Pifas?"

The little ghost frowned, trying to understand. "I like it, but I am kind of used to my long and fancy name," he argued.

"Oh, that's still your name," explained Ruy. "Look, 'P' for Plutarch, 'I' for Ignatius, 'F' for Francis, 'A' for Anthony, and 'S' for Sebastian. P-I-F-A-S. Pifas."

"Oh, that's great! I really like that!" said the very happy ghost.

They shook hands on it, and Ruy said, "Okay, now its bedtime. I'm really tired."

Pifas looked at him a little sad and said, "We ghosts don't sleep at night. We sleep during the day. At night we play. Let's play, Ruy Diver!"

"Oh, no," answered Ruy, after a huge yawn. "I sleep at night and play during the day."

"Oh, all right," said Pifas, already peeking out the window. "I can play in this wonderful place you brought me to. You can use my bed while I'm playing, and I'll sleep during your playtime." That sounded reasonable to both of them.

However, Pifas said, "I need a hiding place. All ghosts need one," and started peeking around the house.

Ruy Diver went to his closet and opened the door. Pifas flew in, absolutely overjoyed. "This is what I've been looking for, for the past three hundred years!" he shouted from the inside.

In a sudden draft, Pifas went to the bed, digging in the feathers and looking for his ghost sheets. He held up two white ones and an orange-colored one for Ruy Diver to admire. He was very proud of the orange one and said, "This is my favorite costume. It's what I wear at parties."

In another draft of wind, Pifas was back in the closet, hanging up his sheets as he said, "Go to sleep, Ruy Diver. I'll be taking care of you during the night."

"That is really nice of you," answered Ruy as he climbed back into bed. "Take care. Have a good time tonight, and I'll see you tomorrow."

Pifas watched the boy fall asleep and felt so fortunate that Ruy Diver was not afraid of him.

And Ruy also smiled in his sleep, thinking how fortunate he was to have another friend.

A VERY DANGEROUS PRANK

The following morning, Ruy Diver woke up early, as it was cleaning day. Once he finished, he went out on the balcony and said good morning to the Ocean. The crabs were already dragging up the bags of oysters and clams.

"Where is everybody?" he asked them.

"We all have to clean house today," they said. "The others sent a message: Everyone is meeting at ten o'clock at the Pearly Fields for another baseball game." Having relayed their message, the crabs went home.

It was still early. Maybe he could help his friends finish up their chores. He put on his diving equipment and jumped into the water.

In no time at all, he was in Rosy Turtle's front yard. But no one was home. Maybe Mr. and Mrs. Turtle had gone food hunting. Where could Rosy be?

Slowly, he swam along, looking left and right until he arrived at Octi Octopus' house among the huge rocks and found him in his front yard, spinning his eight arms like a cartwheel, trying to get the sand away from the front entrance.

But the tide kept pushing the sand back, and all the work Octi had done was useless.

"Can I help you?" asked Ruy Diver.

"No, no, no, no! I'll be finished in no time," Octi answered, busily spinning his arms again. "Are you heading for the Pearly Fields for our game?" he asked, a little breathless.

"Well, I'm looking for Rosy. Have you seen her?" Ruy asked.

"Too busy to see what's going on around me," said Octi.

"If you see her, let her know I'll be at Sally Snapper's," said Ruy.

At the Snapper home, everything had been cleaned and looked orderly. Sally saw Ruy and came toward him, showing off her newly curled curls down her back. She looked lovely.

"What do you think of my new look?" she asked him.

"Great! Just as always, Sally," he answered, adding, "By the way, have you seen Rosy Turtle?"

Sally's smile disappeared, and she pouted. "You always prefer Rosy. That's not fair!" she complained.

Ruy felt bad that he had hurt Sally's feelings, so he took her in his arms and patted her. "No, Sally, I love you all with all my heart, but I worry about Rosy. You know how forgetful she is. You remember that time when she fell asleep for weeks because she forgot to wake up?"

"You are so right!" Sally exclaimed, forgetting her hurt feelings. "Let's go pick up Pete Pompano and look for her."

The search continued until Sarah Sardine suddenly zipped by.

"Sarah, have you seen Rosy Turtle?" they called out.

Sarah zipped back as fast as she had passed them. "Yes! Yes, I saw her quite a while ago eating grass at the Lagoon Fields."

"Thank you, Sarah," said a very relieved Ruy Diver. "Tell everyone I'm ready to meet them at the Pearly Fields for our game."

Heading for the Lagoon Fields, Sarah disappeared, leaving behind a silver wake as if she were competing in a swimming match.

Finally, they all reached the beautiful fields of tender, bright green grass. The only other fish playing around were the ones who lived in this neighborhood, plus Sarah Sardine, who was zipping from one place to another.

"How strange, I can't see her, she's not here" said Sarah. "Rosy! Rosy Turtle, where are you?" she called.

There was no answer.

Suddenly, she saw something was different about the flat Lagoon Fields. She knew the place well and couldn't remember seeing a stack of stones in the middle of the field.

Hmmm, how and when did these stones move over here? She asked herself. She inspected them up close and saw tiny bubbles coming through the cracks between the stones. Each bubble burst, letting out a tiny voice that said, "Help … help … please … someone … help me …"

It was Rosy's voice! But where was she?

"Rosy, Rosy, where are you?" cried out Ruy Diver, worried sick.

"Help … I'm drowning!" said the breaking bubble carrying Rosy's voice.

How could Ruy help her, his very best friend, if he could not even see her?

The bubbles became smaller and smaller, and the voice weakened.

"Here … under … the … stones …"

Losing no time, Ruy grabbed one stone, another, another, two, three… The bubbles got smaller and smaller, and now they burst with no voice at all.

At last he saw her. Soon she would be free! One more stone, another huge one. He pulled and pushed with all his might, but the stones wouldn't move. The bubbles ceased.

"Rosy is dying!" he shouted, and with one last great push, he finally dislodged the huge stone that kept her prisoner.

There she was, the poor thing, her neck stretched out and her head lying on the sand, with her pinkish tongue dangling out of the side of her mouth. Her beautiful long-lashed eyes were closed.

"Rosy, Rosy, speak to me!" begged Ruy. "Please, Rosy, say something!"

Rosy couldn't answer.

With the greatest tenderness, Ruy Diver took her in his arms and swam up to the surface as fast as he could.

Once on the beach, exhausted from the monumental effort he had made to remove the stones, he lay on the sand with Rosy Turtle in his arms. Once he caught his breath, he turned her on her back and gave her mouth-to-mouth resuscitation. Rosy started coughing and spitting water, and then she began to breathe evenly. Both of them exhausted, they lay quietly on the sand, holding hands.

Later, much later, Rosy Turtle said in a soft, weak voice, "Thank you, Ruy. You saved my life."

Now Ruy Diver began to feel a great anger bubbling inside of him. Who could have done such a horrible thing to someone as nice as Rosy Turtle?

"How did this happen, Rosy?" he asked.

And she began to tell him. She had woken up very early and was feeling very hungry. Her mom and dad had already gone to Aunt Cookie's house to have breakfast, and she decided to go on her own to eat the lovely, tender green grass at the Lagoon Fields. She wanted to be really strong for the baseball game. She was eating when Filbert Shark came up to her, saying he would keep her company. He didn't eat anything; he only stared at her with a sneaky smile on his face. He kept insisting that she eat more and more … and she ate it. She really stuffed herself up and was beginning to feel sleepy, so she fell asleep.

Oh, blessed Saint Mermaid! When she awoke, she was surrounded by darkness like it was nighttime. She even thought she had slept all day long.

"When I tried to go home," she said, ending her story, "I couldn't move."

Ruy Diver was stunned by the horrible story and suspected already who had done such a dangerous, awful, ugly thing to his very best friend.

"I think Filbert Shark has gone beyond reasonable limits," he concluded.

Remembering he had made arrangements to meet at the Pearly Fields for the baseball game, he asked Rosy if she felt up to going and telling them the game was cancelled. She agreed.

What chattering, mumbling, prattling, and gibble-gabble met them upon arrival at the Pearly Fields! Everyone was upset and immediately relieved on seeing Rosy Turtle.

"That was the last straw!" cried out Sarah Sardine.

"Absolutely intolerable!" added Octi Octopus. His huge head was bright red, he was so angry.

"I'm totally sick and tired of this stupid behavior!" said Sally Snapper.

"It's not fair!" cried out Sarah Sardine again.

"Hold it. Hold it just a minute," said a very serious Ruy Diver. "We're sorry for getting here so late—" but he was interrupted by Pete Pompano, who said very seriously:

"This is the limit. We will take it no more."

"Let me explain," said Ruy.

"Foolish and stubborn!" exclaimed Joey Fish.

"Hey, you guys, let me explain," insisted Ruy Diver, who thought they were reprimanding him for having arrived so late.

"You don't need to explain, Ruy Diver," said Octi, raising his arms and calling for time out. He began to explain what had happened that made them so upset.

It turned out that Filbert Shark had come around when they were warming up for the game, tossing the ball around, and he just grabbed the ball, saying he would be the only one batting that day and that all the rest had to take turns pitching to him.

The entire group complained and told him to play fair or go home.

"And what do you think he did?" asked Octi.

Everyone was silent, waiting for Ruy Diver to guess.

He was still thinking about the dangerous prank Filbert had played on Rosy Turtle, and he had to ask what new mischief Filbert had come up with. "What did he do?" he asked.

"He swallowed the ball!" they shouted.

Ruy Diver had to agree with all of them: This was unacceptable behavior. "He's gone too far now. Let's go look for him. There is something else I need to talk about with him, something very dangerous that he's done."

They organized three groups that would go hunt Filbert out. Whoever saw him first would sound the alarm, and the sea snails would trumpet the instructions of where to meet. Once assembled, they would confront Filbert Shark.

Little did they know that Filbert was listening to their plans, hiding behind a huge bunch of seaweed.

Hearing the awful things they were saying about him, his tiny eyes began to fill with tears. He felt horrible and sad because no one liked him. His whole body started shaking with sobs, and his fins were not enough to brush away the waterfall of tears.

"Nobody loves me. Nobody loves me. Poor me! Why don't they love me?" he sobbed and sobbed.

Knowing he would be found sooner or later, he decided to go home to his mom. Swallowing his loneliness, his body all hunched over, he tiptoed home thinking no one had seen him.

Pete Pompano was the first to see him creeping into his cave home and sounded the alert for the sea snails to trumpet out the information.

The group met at Filbert Shark's home in a swarm. What should be the first step?

"Throw stones at him," said Sally Snapper.

"Hit him with the bat!" exclaimed Joey Fish.

"Wait a minute, everybody!" said Ruy Diver wisely. "We don't want revenge. That gets you nowhere and causes more quarreling."

"So right, Ruy Diver. Violence only creates more violence," said Sarah Sardine, surprised at her own wisdom.

"What should we do?" asked Pete, not quite convinced they should be calm about the events.

"I think the first step should be to find out why Filbert did these ugly things," said a very calm Ruy Diver.

Just then, Mrs. Shark opened the front door and saw them all just waiting.

"Good morning, kids. Can I help you?" she greeted.

Ruy said very seriously, "We would like to talk to Filbert."

"Oh, dear." Mrs. Shark suspected there was bad news connected to her precious Filbert. Silently she went in to look for her son. If he had done something wrong, he had to face up to it.

Mr. Shark was reading his newspaper, comfortably seated on the sofa. "Anything wrong, dear?" he asked.

"I think so. Where is Filbert?" she said.

"Try his bedroom," he answered, looking back at the newspaper.

Mrs. Shark didn't see Filbert right away and thought his bedroom was empty, but then she saw his tail sticking out from under the bed.

"What have you been up to, Filbert?" she asked in a serious voice.

"I'm not here. I'm not here," he said.

"You better come out and go fix your problems with your friends," she ordered.

Mr. Shark came in just then. "What is going on? Filbert, come out, now!" he said in a loud voice.

Filbert crawled out from under his bed, arguing his defense. "I didn't cover Rosy Turtle with stones when she fell asleep, and I did not swallow the ball," he said in a shaky, guilty tone.

"If you didn't do all this, why are you so scared?" said Mr. Shark, taking Filbert by a fin and pulling him out the front door to face the very serious crowd that waited for him.

Filbert cringed and wiggled as he lowered his head, expecting a shower of knocks and blows. When he peeped at Ruy Diver from under his protective fin and saw that the boy was just staring at him, not in anger, not in reproach, just looking at him, he felt confused.

"Did you cover Rosy Turtle with stones?" asked Ruy.

"No, no, no. It wasn't me!" said Filbert, very scared.

"Filbert, the truth will always shine," warned Ruy Diver.

"Well, I was—we were—I was playing with her. I thought it would be a great prank," confessed Filbert.

Rosy Turtle was very angry. She came forward to face Filbert.

"You, brat! You silly, stupid brat!" she shouted. "I could have died!"

Filbert Shark hung his head, realizing that, indeed, he had done something very dangerous to someone as harmless as Rosy. He felt really bad.

"I'm sorry, Rosy," he said humbly.

"And what about our ball?" shouted Joey Fish.

Again, Filbert Shark curled up on himself, whispering, "I don't have it."

"Liar!" shouted the group.

"It's true!" he whimpered. "I don't have it anymore. My stomach has it."

Now, this was a problem, a big problem. There was only one ball. That meant no more baseball games.

Suddenly, Filbert Shark stretched himself out, as long as he was, and a glimmer of an intelligent idea shone in his tiny, nearly blind eyes.

"I'll ask my dad to shake me by the tail, upside down, until the ball comes out!" he exclaimed.

"Yes! Way to go! Yes!" they all encouraged him.

"Dad! Help! Help me!" shouted Filbert.

Mr. Shark was out in an instant, thinking his son was in danger or being hurt by the mob that had come looking for his baby boy.

"What! What's going on here?" he anxiously demanded.

"Grab my tail and shake me upside down, so the ball comes out!" said Filbert.

Mr. Shark squinted his tiny eyes at his son. "I thought you said you didn't have it," he said.

"Dad, the truth always shines," said Filbert.

The ball rolled out in two shakes. Octi Octopus stretched out one of his arms, grabbed the ball, and raced off to the Pearly Fields, followed by everyone else.

Ruy Diver held on to one of Filbert's fins, saying quietly, "You and I have to talk."

They stayed behind, Filbert waiting with a lowered head for a harsh scolding from Ruy Diver. He knew he had done something very bad, very dangerous for someone else. What could he say, except that he was really sorry for being so thoughtless?

However, Ruy Diver did not scold him. He simply asked, "Do you think you could consider the consequences of your silly, dangerous pranks?"

"Thank you, Ruy Diver. I will really think about this: consequences."

And off they went for a good game at the Pearly Fields.

THE END FOR NOW!

CPSIA information can be obtained
at www.ICGtesting.com
Printed in the USA
LVIC061741190613
339361LV00002B

9 781481 754774